THE NERVOUS SYSTEM

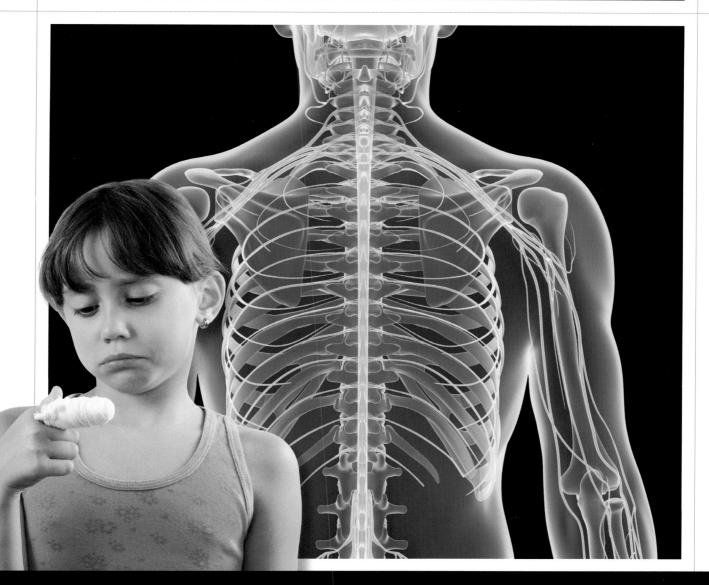

BY SUSAN H. GRAY

Published by The Child's World®
1980 Lookout Drive • Mankato, MN 56003-1705
800-599-READ • www.childsworld.com

Acknowledgments
The Child's World®: Mary Berendes, Publishing Director
Red Line Editorial: Editorial direction
The Design Lab: Design
Amnet: Production

Content Consultant: R. John Solaro, Ph.D., Distinguished
University Professor and Head, Department of Physiology and
Biophysics, University of Illinois Chicago

Photographs ©: Sebastian Kaulitzki/Shutterstock Images, cover
(background), 1 (background); Shutterstock Images, cover
(foreground), 1 (foreground); Wavebreak Media/Thinkstock,
4, 14; iStockphoto/Thinkstock, 7, 10, 16; Jupiter Images/
Thinkstock, 8; Fuse/Thinkstock, 13; Digital Vision/Thinkstock, 19;
Blend Images/Thinkstock, 21

ISBN 9781626873377
LCCN 2014930674

Printed in the United States of America
Mankato, MN
July, 2014
PA02221

ABOUT THE AUTHOR

Susan H. Gray has a bachelor's and a master's degree in zoology. In her 25 years as an author, she has written many medical articles, grant proposals, and children's books. Ms. Gray and her husband, Michael, live in Cabot, Arkansas.

TABLE OF CONTENTS

CHAPTER 1

Blasting Away

Michael was really hot. Today, he was beating everybody at video games. His eyes darted back and forth. He missed nothing on the screen. His fingers were wrapped tightly around the controller.

Your nervous system helps you do many things every day, including playing video games.

He punched its button with a sharp jab. An asteroid blasted out of the sky.

Another asteroid popped up on the screen. Special nerve cells in Michael's eyes spotted it. Other cells picked up the asteroid's bright blue color. The cells shot a message to Michael's brain: "There's something on the screen!" In the brain, other cells got the signal: "It's an asteroid! Blast it!" The cells zoomed the signal down Michael's neck and out to his arm. Muscles in his thumb got the message. Michael punched the controller button. The asteroid blew to bits.

Everything happened in a split second. Michael's thumb jabbed the button almost as soon as his eyes saw the asteroid. His nerves and muscles worked together. They reacted in a flash. And Michael racked up another 500 points.

CHAPTER 2

What Is the Nervous System?

The nervous system is a group of cells reaching the whole body. Special parts of the cells sense things in the **environment**. They pick up light, sound, pressure, and temperature. Other parts of the cells cause the body to react. They make you blink, grin, and press a controller button.

The nervous system is made up of two parts. They are the central nervous system and the peripheral nervous system. The central nervous system includes the brain and the spinal cord. In an adult, the brain weighs about 3 pounds (1.36 kg). The spinal cord is a bundle of nerve cells. It starts at the base of the brain and runs down the back. **Vertebrae** surround and protect it. In an adult, the spinal cord is about 18 inches (46 cm) long.

The peripheral nervous system is made up of all the other nerves in the body. It includes nerves running

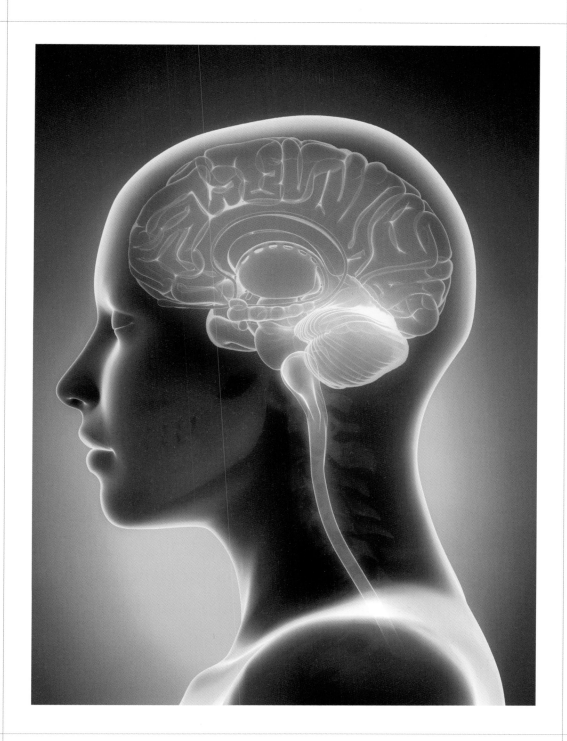

The brain is a soft mass of nerve tissue in the skull.

from the ears to the brain. It includes nerves going from the spinal cord out to the fingertips. It even includes nerves that lead to the heart and lungs.

People can control the actions of some nerves. Actions you can control are called voluntary actions. You can control the nerves that make your legs run. Your brain can decide to do these things. Then your nervous system makes them happen.

Some of the body's activities happen automatically. These are called involuntary actions. You do not have to think about these activities for them to happen. But the nervous system still controls them. You don't have to lie awake at night remembering to breathe. Nerves to the lungs take care of this.

You can control the nerves that make your mouth chew gum.

CHAPTER 3

What Is a Nerve Cell?

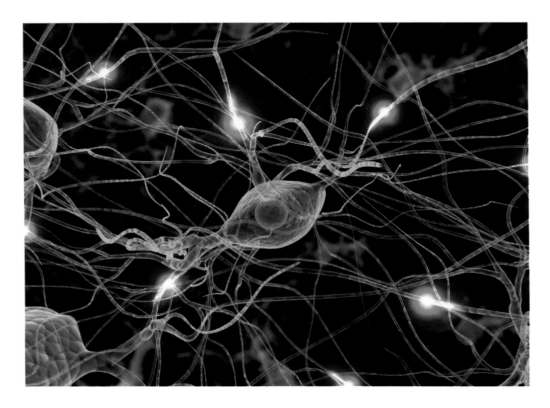

The nervous system is made up of millions of nerve cells. Nerve cells are also called neurons. Some neurons are very short. They might run only from one part of the brain to another. Other neurons are much longer. These might run from the spinal

Neurons come in many sizes and run to different areas of the body.

cord all the way down to the toes.

A nerve cell, or neuron, has three main parts. They are the **dendrites**, the cell body, and the **axon**. Most nerve cells have several dendrites. These are short, little hair-like branches. They lead to the cell body. The cell body is an enlarged part of the neuron. It is often star-shaped. An axon extends from the cell body. In many neurons, the axon runs out to end at the muscle cells. In others, the axon meets dendrites of another neuron.

CHAPTER 4

How Does the Nervous System Work?

The nervous system works by picking up messages and making the body respond. Some messages go to the brain. Other messages leave from the brain. Nerves in your hand might send a message to the brain when they sense a pinprick. Your brain sends a message telling the mouth to say "Ouch!" Nerve endings in the skin, eyes, ears, nose, and tongue pick up messages. Nerve endings deep inside the body also pick up messages.

The dendrites pick up the signals first. The ends of some dendrites are built to pick up heat, cold, or touch. Some are built to pick up light, color, sound, smell, or taste. Dendrites then send their signals to the cell and axon. They send these signals as electricity.

The electricity speeds down the axon to the central nervous system.

In the central nervous system, other nerves translate the messages. They figure out how the body should react. The brain or spinal cord shoots electrical signals down other nerves. These signals zoom out to body parts, telling them what to do. The nerve endings release chemicals to these body parts.

When you smell a flower, nerve endings in your nose pick up the message.

The chemicals make muscles move. They make you jump away from danger. They make you punch a controller button.

In many cases, the nerve signals pass through the brain and spinal cord. But in some cases, they only pass through the spinal cord.

Nerves that only go to the spinal cord are called the reflex pathways. Reflexes help us in times of danger.

When you visit the doctor, they check your reflexes to make sure your nerve signals are working.

Suppose you touch a hot iron. Suddenly your hand jerks back. Here, nerves in your fingers sent signals to the spinal cord. Then nerves in the spinal cord sent signals right to your arm. They made your arm and hand pull away from danger. The signals did not have to travel all the way to the brain. This allowed you to escape danger more quickly.

CHAPTER 5

What about the Senses?

People have five senses. These are sight, hearing, smell, taste, and touch. Senses tell us about the environment around us. The body has special nerve cells that pick up information about the environment. Many of these cells are in the eyes, ears, nose, tongue, and skin.

Nerve cells in the eyes send pictures to the brain.

More than 100 million special cells in the retina pick up light and color. Neurons in the brain figure out the meanings of the pictures. Some of

the eye cells pick up different colors. People who are colorblind are often missing some of these eye cells. They cannot tell the difference between some colors.

Cells deep inside the ear pick up vibrations from sound waves. They send the vibrations to the brain. The brain sorts out their meanings.

Cells in the nose pick up different smells in the air. The brain interprets the chemical messages. Human beings have about 40 million nose cells.

Taste buds on the tongue also pick up chemicals. Taste buds are little bundles of cells. The average person has about 10,000 taste buds.

CHAPTER 6

Keeping the Nervous System Healthy

The nervous system works properly in most people. This is because it gets plenty of oxygen from the blood. It also gets the proper nutrients. Foods such as chicken and fish contain the protein needed to make nerve chemicals. Bread, pasta, and fruit provide the sugar for energy. And vitamin B12, found in eggs and milk, helps to build and strengthen the nerve cells.

Some diseases keep the nervous system from doing its job. Alzheimer's disease often affects older people. Those who have Alzheimer's disease begin to have trouble remembering simple facts. Over time, they may not be able to make decisions or even recognize their own family members. Some scientists think

*Eating healthy will help take care of
the nervous system.*

Alzheimer's may be caused by clumps called tangles inside the brain's neurons. They still have many questions about Alzheimer's. But scientists think that keeping your mind and body active your whole life may help you avoid this disease.

A blood clot in the brain can also cause serious problems for the nervous system. The clot keeps blood from getting to the nerve cells. The cells then fail to get enough oxygen or nutrients. After a few minutes, neurons start to die. If certain neurons die, a person may forget where he or she lives. If other cells die, the person could lose their sense of smell. If still other cells die, the person could have trouble moving or talking. When oxygen and nutrients cannot reach brain cells, a person is said to have a stroke.

Usually the nervous system works properly, though. Every second, it shoots messages all over the body. It stays busy without us knowing, even as we sleep. The nervous system is truly amazing.

The nervous system is always working and sending messages, even when we least expect it!

GLOSSARY

axon (AKS-on) An axon is a long and single process of a neuron that carries impulses away from the cell body. An axon extends from the cell body.

dendrites (DEN-drights) Dendrites are branching extensions of a neuron through which impulses travel toward the cell body. Most nerve cells have several dendrites.

detect (di-TEKT) To detect something is to discover or sense it. Some people's nervous systems do not detect pain.

environment (en-VYE-ruhn-muhnt) The environment is a living creature's surroundings. Senses tell us about our environment.

sciatic nerves (SI-a-tik NURVS) The sciatic nerves are nerves that run down the back of the legs. The sciatic nerves are the largest nerves in the body.

vertebrae (VUR-tuh-bray) Vertebrae are one of the sections of bone or cartilage that make up the spinal column. Vertebrae surround and protect the spinal cord.

LEARN MORE

BOOKS

Burstein, John. *The Astounding Nervous System.*
New York: Crabtree Publishing, 2009.

Gardner, Jane P. *Take a Closer Look at Your Brain.*
Mankato, MN: The Child's World, 2014.

Manolis, Kay. *The Nervous System.*
Minneapolis: Bellwether Media, 2009.

WEB SITES

Visit our Web site for links about the nervous system:
childsworld.com/links

Note to Parents, Teachers, and Librarians: We routinely verify our Web links to make sure they are safe and active sites. So encourage your readers to check them out!

INDEX